Laurence King

Published in 2000 by Laurence King Publishing
an imprint of Calmann & King Ltd
71 Great Russell Street
London WC1B 3BN
Tel: +44 20 7831 6351
Fax: +44 20 7831 8356
e-mail: enquiries@calmann-king.co.uk
www.laurence-king.com

Distributed in the United States and Canada by
te Neues Publishing Company
16 West 22nd Street
New York, New York 10010
Tel: 212 627 9090
Fax: 212 627 9511
www.teneues.com

A catalogue record for this book is available from the British Library.

UK ISBN 1 85669 192 6
US ISBN 3-8238-5462-3

Printed in Hong Kong

Fuel Three Thousand

Peter Miles Damon Murray Stephen Sorrell

Text
Shannan Peckham

1.

Anatomy

The history of depth is inseparable from the history of vision. Definitions of depth have shifted with technological innovations. The use of the microscope and the invention of the X-ray, for example, formed part of a nineteenth-century revolution in visual technology that transformed surfaces into depths, even as depth was made to surface. These transformations shaped the way individuals observed themselves in the world.

The word 'sur-face' points to a connection between the human body and concepts of depth. The body is imagined as an interior space. The physician strives to bring to light the hidden secrets within it. In the fifteenth century anatomists endeavoured to map the interior of the body beneath the skin through analogies with the perilous explorations of the New World. Individuals had concealed territories within them that need colonising.

Depth means time. As the archaeologist burrows below the surface, into the bowels of the earth, so he moves backwards through history to claim a buried pre-history. This process of temporal regression has been conceptualised as a return to some authentic and immutable golden age preserved below the vicissitudes of the shallow life above. At other times, the archaeologist's uncovering of the primitive past is construed as a violation, or a dangerous introspection that exposes him to a vestigial barbarism. Depth is a place to be sought after and a dark place to be feared.

The notions of depth and digging, as they have been developed through archaeology's engagement with material culture, have also been applied figuratively to describe other processes. Reading is imagined as an archaeological practice. Scriptural writings, with their weighty metaphorical language, promoted the idea of reading as a moral enterprise whereby concealed meanings were recuperated through the exertions of the earnest reader or listener. Reading, in this sense, involved the retrieval of a buried knowledge from a subtext. The profundity of a reader was gauged by the extent to which he could fathom the inner recesses of the text.

Archaeological ideas of retrieval have been developed most fully in psychoanalytic notions of depth. The unconscious, for example, is conceived as a depth, while the analyst has been likened to an archaeologist excavating beneath the individual's surface consciousness. The analyst disinters buried experiences and in the process brings the patient back to the world from the depths of despair. The surface signifies a line of demarcation that separates the visible from the hidden, the private from the public. A 'breakdown', in psychological terms, denotes the collapse of any separation so that latent anxieties erupt through the surface into the outside world.

Depth was promoted in the late nineteenth century as an antidote to the destabilising flow of commodities over the surface of the globe. The city became linked to the underground, imagined as a place where people were being buried under the weight of new and alienating technologies. The dangers of the superficial had to be stemmed by uncovering 'the hidden abode of production' to show how capital produced and was, in turn, produced.

Even though ways of seeing have changed through time, cultures have always read the world vertically: the Heavens above, the Earth, and the Underworld, the

These different, but related concepts of depth, draw upon ancient narratives that dramatise the quest for truth as a gruelling journey underground. 'Insight' here is literalised as a descent into the earth. In classical mythology, the hero descends into the underworld that is a place of torment, just as the subterranean world in the Christian imagination is evoked as a realm of horror.

Conscious and the Unconscious.

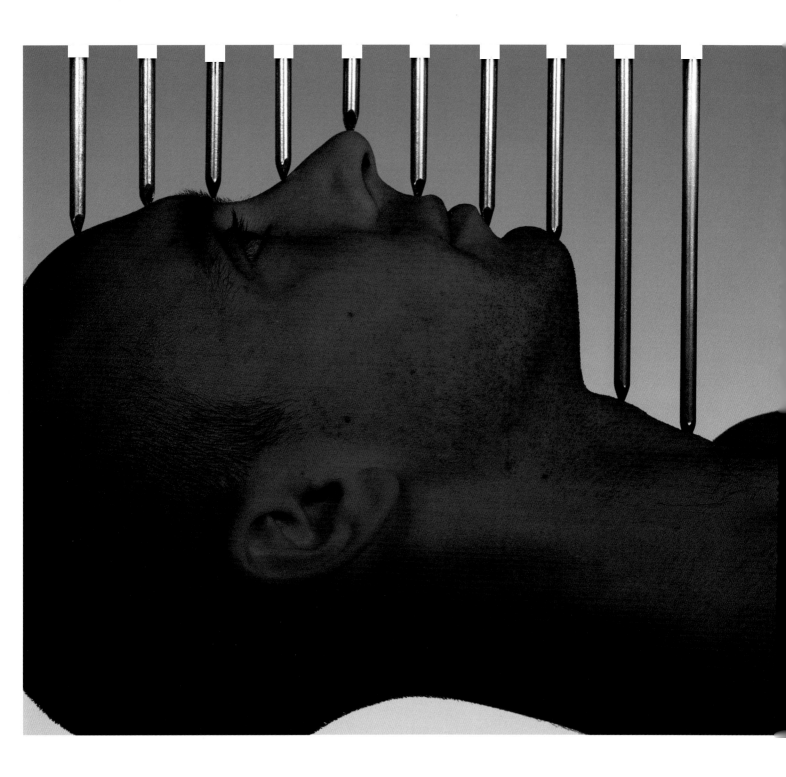

They made the things they saw
Whatever was pictured beyond this sight
Became the blindness that let them see.

Passer-by, think of them when you find
The invisible signature they left
On the world you have brought to light.

THEY MADE

THE THINGS

THEY SAW

THEIR END

WAS TO IMAGINE

A BEGINNING

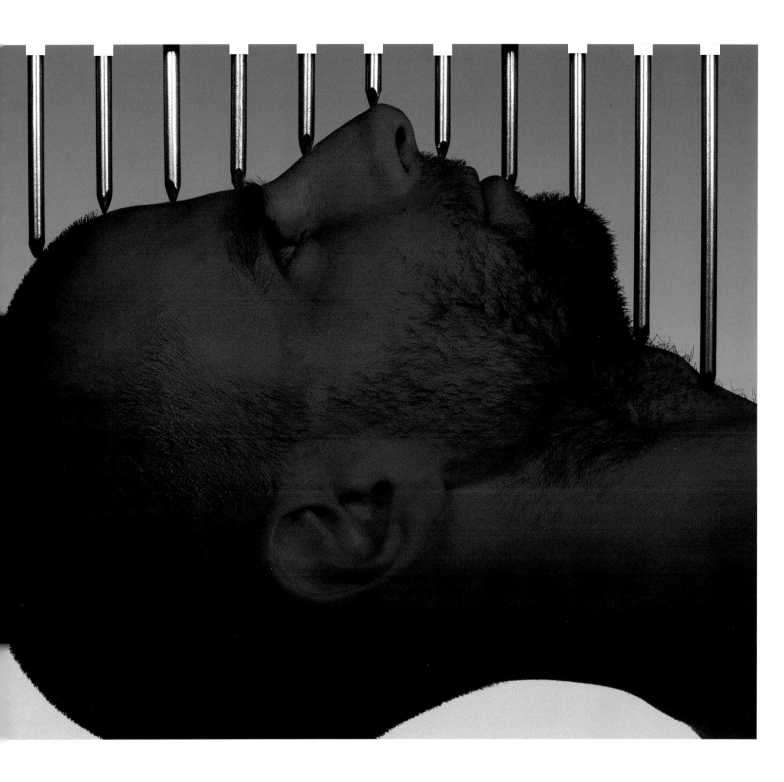

Their end was to imagine a beginning
That had no history other than the present
From which it was imagined.

Passer-by, remember them when you forget,
As you sometimes must,
Why you set out on this walk in the beginning.

Others sat down
at the table they had set
But only they could choose what was eaten.

Passer-by, think of them when you have lost
Your way among the endless choices
And are waiting for a sign.

AND ARE WAITING

FOR A SIGN

1. Wood

The highroad of a sentence
is a belt that straps the wood together.
On either side, paths disappear into
the limelight of vegetating distractions.
This is the moving pavement that
her eye travels along, playing with
the possibility of diversions.

The walker invents the stories as she
goes, painting her way with blue
arrows. When everything in her bag[2]
has been used once, the hush returns
to its original eloquence.

2. Baggage

There is a limit to what she can take on journey, even though she needs to be prepared r every eventuality. Unpacking articles in ifferent places brings exotic meanings to their miliarity. Baggage is not to be left unattended hen she travels, otherwise it runs the risk of eing destroyed. Things can be lost in suitcases, uried[3] among the commonplace; that is hy they are the perfect space to smuggle the nacceptable face of her conformity.

3. Burial

It takes effort and time to bury something, it has to be worthwhile. Burial is her way of cking and unpacking in one. She hides the ings that should be kept out of sight and marks[4] e site where they first became invisible. Burial is ground where she has to tread softly, otherwise e might undo what she has already done.

Markers

Orange buoys mark the places where people ve gone after her. They are inflated cryptograms, mpkin heads hollowed out into angry signs it point to the gravity of their own warning. Only e unsinkable can show up a wrecked visibility.[5] e looks up at the muscular underside of the ry as it sails by loaded with its unlikely ending. neath the commotion she is as calm as the water, there is no need to come up for air.

Visibility

The more closely she looks at something, the re chaotic it appears. Individuals become a crowd en she observes them from a distance and they shrink fleshy abstraction when she sees them too closely. e knows she has arrived when she can tell the wood[1] m the trees. To save something, she has to remember v it looked the moment she committed it to memory. en the fire licks the visible, all the invisible animals de come screaming into the open.

A fruit that can be sliced open, the pithy flesh puckering under the knife. You could choke on these seeds if you didn't know how to prepare it.

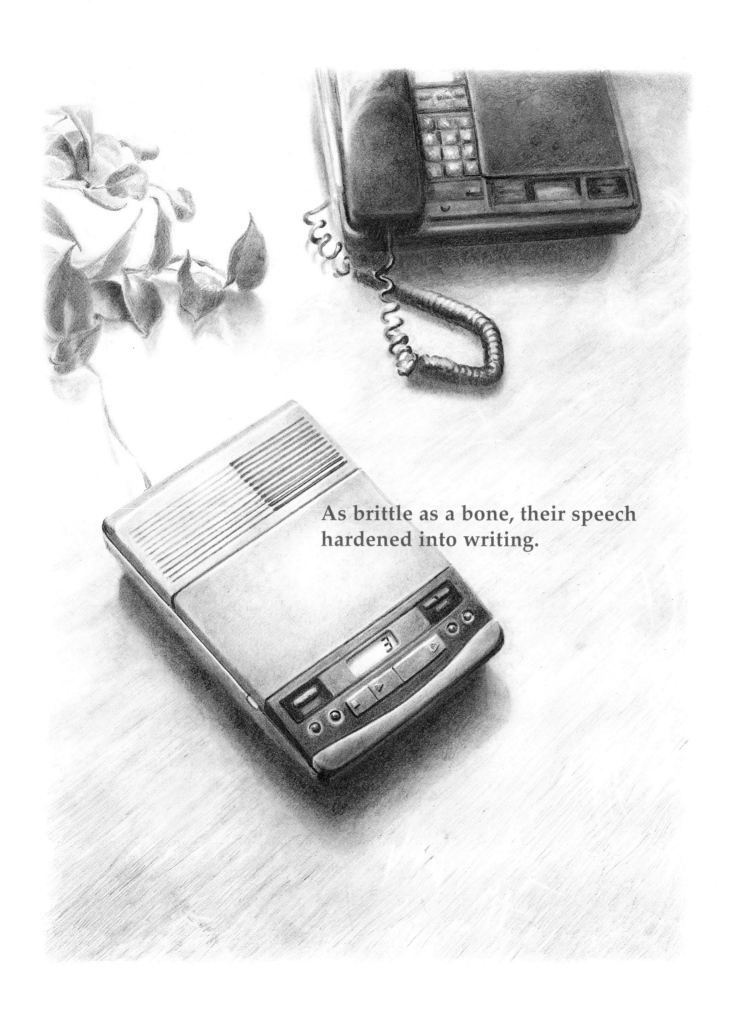

As brittle as a bone, their speech
hardened into writing.

As chewed-up as bubble-gum
glued under the table,
miniature memorials to a
mechanical resentment that
hardens on the underside
of conversations.

It was too late by the time she understood that a jealous woman never recognises herself.

He looked at everything
with suspicion, but he was
most distrustful of the things
he couldn't see.

Behind closed doors they
were conspiring against him.
His jealousy would end, he
thought, if he could prove to
the world that it was true.

A wound that's been stitched up and healed with a scar that only the sharpest eyes can see when the light is right, or receptive fingers when they're playing the tune.

It moved inside
her body, as material
as the food she ate.

It requires strength to blow up into the shape you want, ballooning overnight into a comfortable obsession and then shrinking back into its inflatable beginnings.

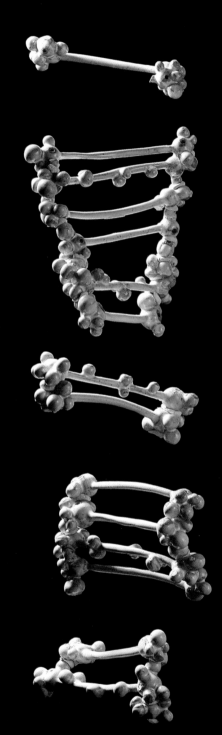

...cause the body (every body) could
...opened up at any moment and tuned
...the perfect A.

...d around us, inside us, the humming
...machines like tiny bouncy spy-planes
...invisible proximity mapping out the
...solute sprawl of a city, or the neat
...mmed cartoon hedges of a speculator.

A game of
pass the parcel
that's played
for the prize of
unwrapping.

Nobody cares
what's on the inside
if the outside
reflects what they
want to see.

This game began the moment you chose to play it.

What does the perfect choice look like?

A bisected artichoke with its leaves around a heart.

A pantomime horse with two heads, arriving everywhere and nowhere to applause.

A table that's set for one with two people expecting to eat.

A mouth that's reading another mouth to know how it should settle.

A word that's spoken as if it was a question that contained an answer.

A lie that's told to explain the inexplicable.

A juggler's hands that freeze for a moment while they gather their strength.

A man who is holding out his clenched fists and asks where the money's hidden.

A new pair of shoes that hurt when you walk, so you stand as still as a scarecrow.

The cost of other people's choices is always higher than our own.

Choosing, like breathing, becomes harder when you think about it.

The end of one choice is the beginning of another one.

The choices that are made with the loudest noise aren't made by the people who talk about them loudly.

We only enjoy choosing when we know the outcome doesn't matter.

What would a life without choice look like?

A choice can be mistaken for:

A decision that other people have made to deprive you of a choice.

A game of cards that isn't played for money.

A destiny that didn't exist until the moment you thought you were choosing it.

A belief that's been held so long it's become invisible.

A mirror that reflects whatever you want it to reflect.

A labyrinth where the exit is clearly marked.

A horizon with nothing to frame it.

Someone who loves you for everything you're not.

A language that you're alone in speaking.

A shop that sells everything you don't need.

A sleep that you'll never remember having.

A promise that doesn't have to be kept.

A political system based on true equality.

A robbery where nothing is stolen because the robbers are all rich.

A beginning that ends before it begins.

A lie that's the truth you haven't recognised.

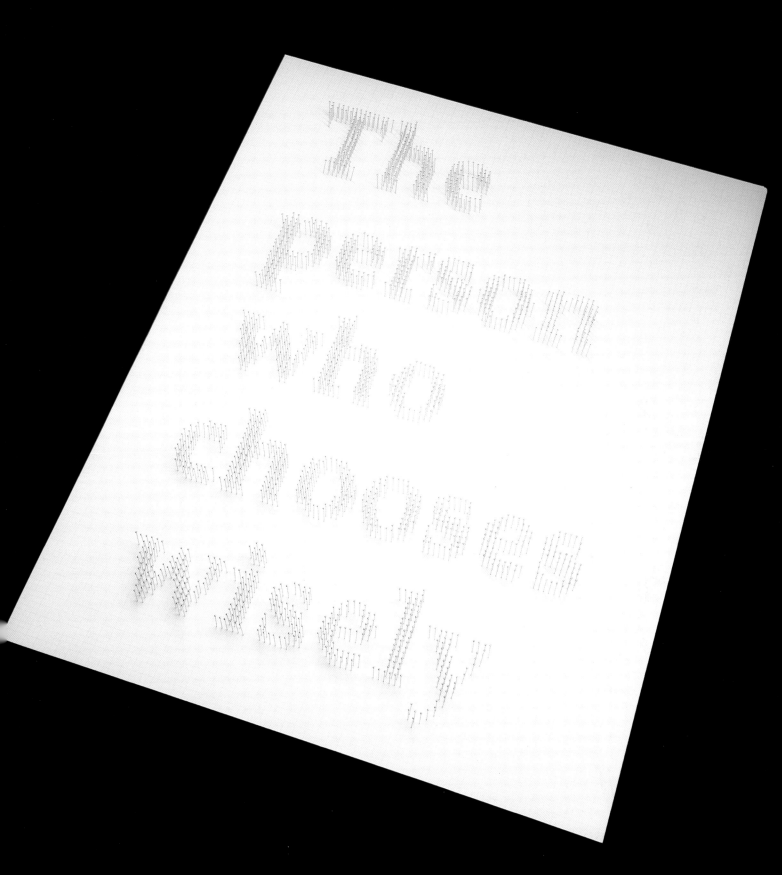

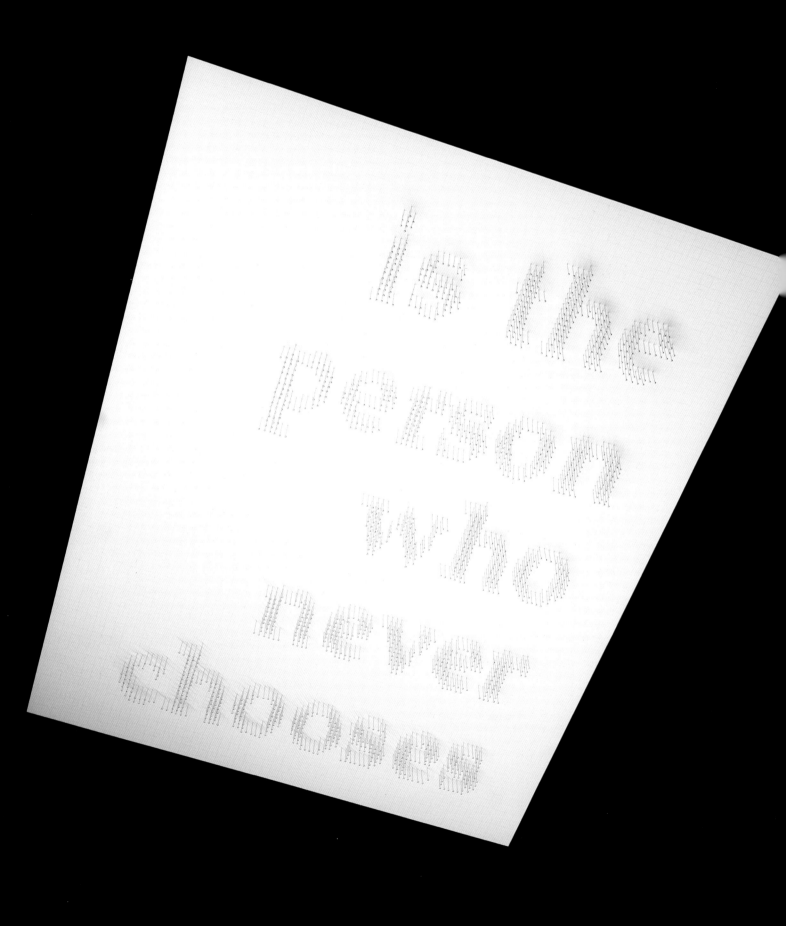

What is the worst choice you have made?

To have played the game with certain knowledge of the consequences.

To have mistaken one choice for another until it was too late.

To have accepted the necessity of choosing without due consideration.

To have thought the right choice was the wrong choice.

To have left before you learned the outcome of your choice.

To have believed that choosing ever made a difference.

What is the best choice you have made?

To have played the game, not knowing what the rules were.

To have conceded that someone else's choice was more important than your own.

To have given up a just reward that didn't satisfy you.

To have been indecisive when the moment called for it.

To have recognised the unimportance of the choice before you made it.

To have kept quiet when others wanted you to speak.

There
are
some
things
beyond
choice,
although
we
choose
not
to
believe
them.

A choice that's made by others for us is never a choice, although it can sometimes be a destiny.

Religion is a belief in the immortality of choice.

A choice that's made unknowingly is called an accident if it turns out to be wrong.

Whatever words we choose there are some things that cannot be said without choosing to ignore others.

Choices are always made, they are never found, although we forget who made them.

You have chosen to look at yourself more carefully than you thought you'd have to.

Wars are the result of incompatible choices.

Choice would be impossible if there was no end to the things we could choose from.

Only silent choices count.

Differences make choices easier.

Faith, for people who believe, is never a choice.

We admire people for the choices that we didn't have the strength to make.

The truth is a choice with an army to enforce it.

The choicest parts are those that get hurt the easiest.

A bad choice is a key that doesn't have a lock to open.

There are more ways than one to choose the same thing.

Sometimes people choose death to overcome the tyranny of living with a choice.

A choice is a memorial to other choices that weren't made.

We know the things we can't choose but we can't choose the things that we don't know.

We are moved by the things we cannot choose: Birth. Love. Illness. Death.

Did you choose to be born?

Love is a choice that isn't recognised, so we imagine it's natural.

A gambler is someone addicted to choice.

Knowledge brings us choices but never the wisdom to choose.

The person who chooses is never the person who is blamed.

Sometimes we choose to forget so that we can remember.

Whatever the value of the object being chosen, it takes the same time to choose.

Choices can only be given to you if they have already been made.

History is the name we give to the choices that we've forgotten.

Paradise was a life without choice; that's why it is impossible to imagine.

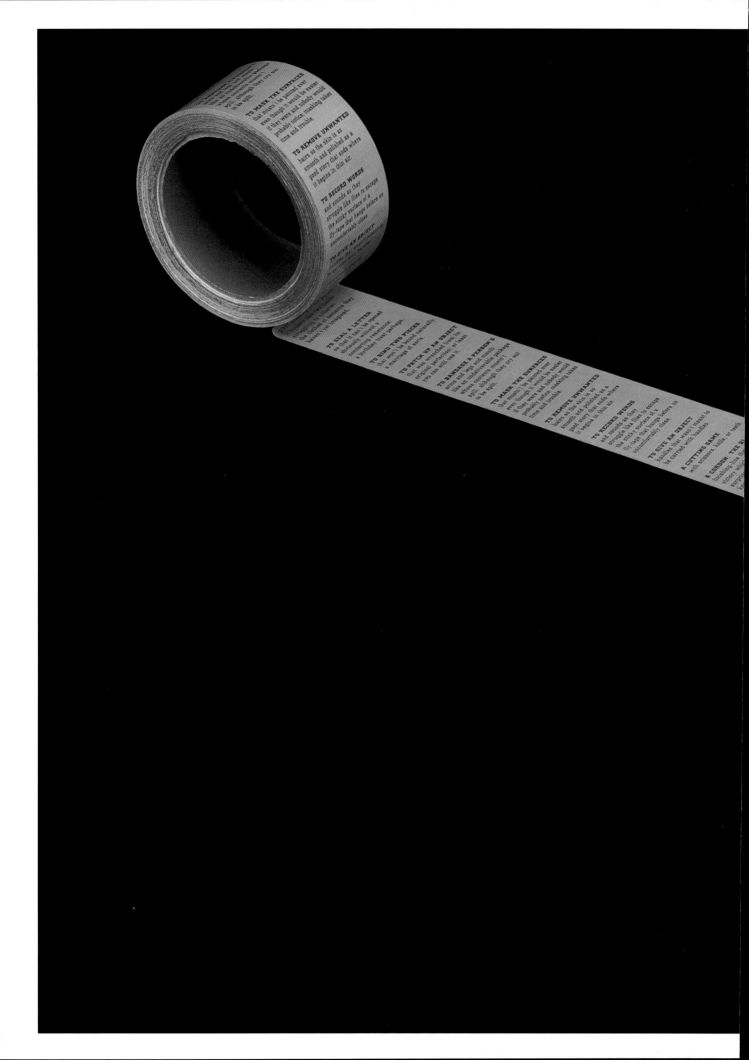

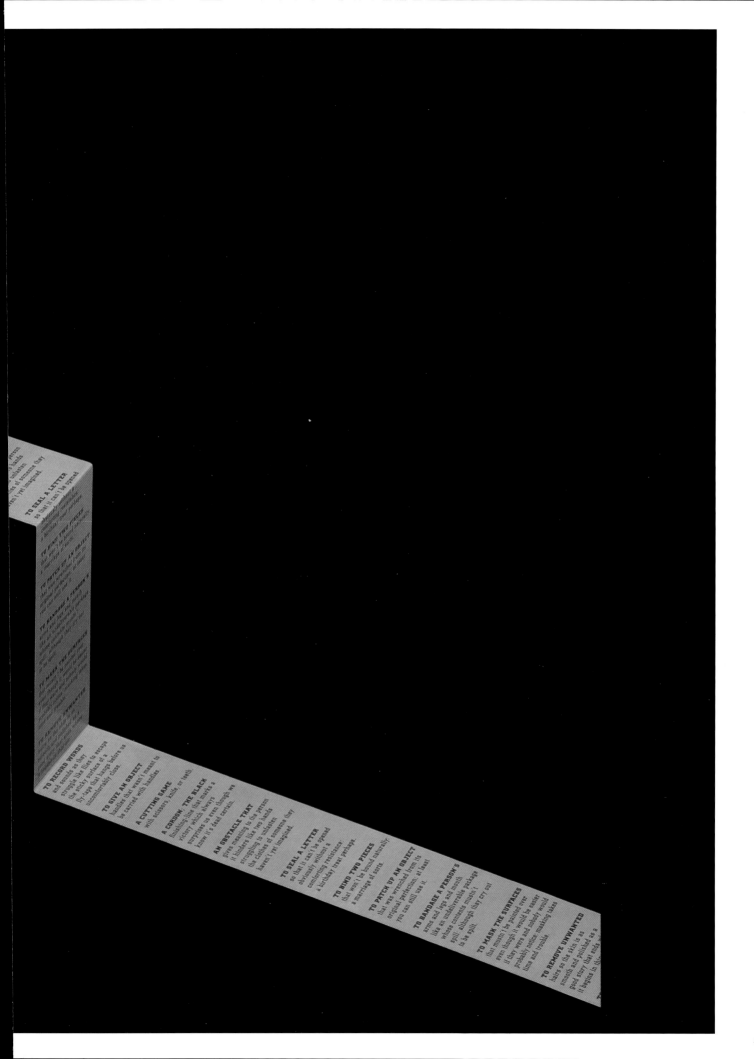

The mirror
is an
eye that
doesn't see
the things
it looks
at,

inverts
truth,
corrects
wrong

the

and

a

Spectacles are both the medium and the object of sight. They are framed lenses that serve to rectify defective vision; but they are also public shows, the object of the sight that is being enhanced. Spectacles were invented in the thirteenth century when the cathedrals were being built with their stained-glass windows; they betokened a new apprehension of the world through glass.

People who wear glasses are identified with erudition, discernment, the focused engagement which intellectual activity entails: writer, money-maker, doctor, priest, psychoanalyst. In some political regimes, the wearers of spectacles have been lauded and in others, they have been persecuted. Spectacles have been construed as a sign of strength or weakness so that the state of the body mirrors the moral condition. On the one hand, glasses intimate commitment to a World View and are emblems of the visionary whose insight enables him to distinguish things that other people cannot see. On the other hand, they suggest a narrow-minded, blinkered vision and have been taken as a visible token of physical infirmity.

The function of spectacles is not only to correct sight, but it is also to protect sight from influences that would otherwise impede the gazer. In theological writings, the Scriptures are conceived as the spectacles without which it would be impossible to look upon the sun. But spectacles also furnish places to hide behind. Perhaps that is why those who wear glasses are often feared. Lenses structure sight. They suggest the parameters within which we gaze upon the world.

Spectacles become metaphors for the ideological enframement and contingency of all vision that may be shattered or violently dislodged by those who see the world differently.

You need to be strong to live inside a fragile house and the people there build their houses completely out of glass.

The buildings rise out of the sand by the sea
like amorphous dreams of our own homes
that have cooled into an implausible rigidity.

The glasshouse is a portal, spectroscope and strongbox in one. You can look at it, or stare through it. When the tide comes in, the glasshouse is an island and the manufactured lucidity of its foundations are concealed by the natural transparency of the sea. The glasshouse radiates a phosphorescent glow at night, like the luminous membrane of a sea creature, that can be seen from a great distance. It is a glass speculum inserted into the fertile body of the world. People move within like embodied gazes through a colossal optical instrument, or abstracted grains of sand in an hourglass. Perspectives are everywhere, so that it is hard to know when to look and where your gaze should finally settle. Everything is exposed and in time, when you grow accustomed to it, the unremitting possibilities of sight become invisible. Glass can be a place to hide, but it is difficult to live discreetly inside an engineered transparency.

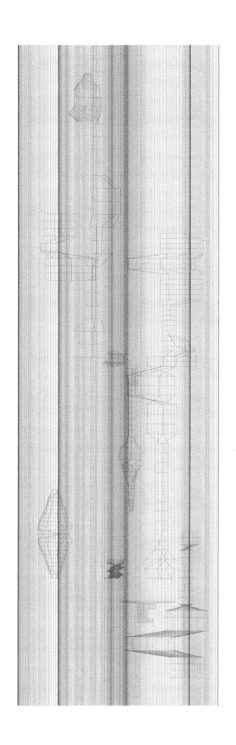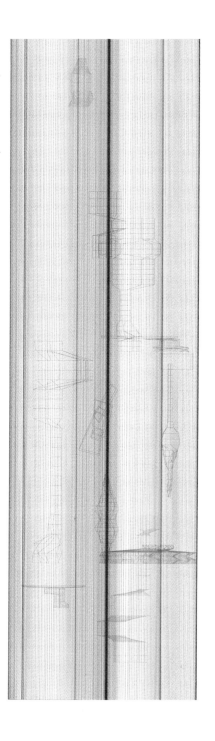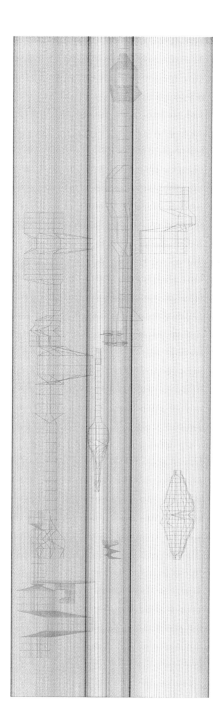

Lives are opened up to view in unexpected ways inside these habitable miracles of glass. It is like moving through the refracted spectrum of a rainbow. Inadvertently, you catch your face reflected back in the transparent surfaces with the glassy world beyond. All relationships are governed by this triangulation: inside, outside and the invisible inbetween.

People lie or sit or stand like the letters of an alphabet that have been captured inside the vitreous breath of a glassblower. The building is an observatory where those inside look out at the world. It is also a spectacle where the observers are displayed to the outside. The inhabitants are exhibitionists and voyeurs who move from room to room as if they were arranging the windows of a department store. Nobody can tell who is seeing whom and whether the glass is a barrier or a conduit to the world they are looking at.

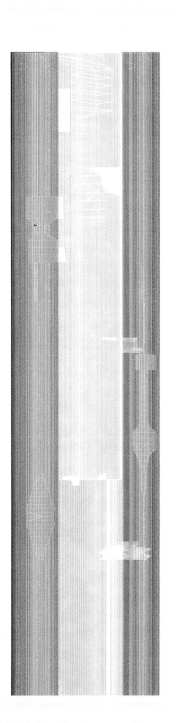

Secrets cannot be hidden in the glasshouse.
Transparency is the moral principle
by which the inhabitants lead their lives,
free from pretence or deceit.

The buildings, like greenhouses, are constructed
to regulate the development of the moral life
within, so that stones won't shatter their lives.

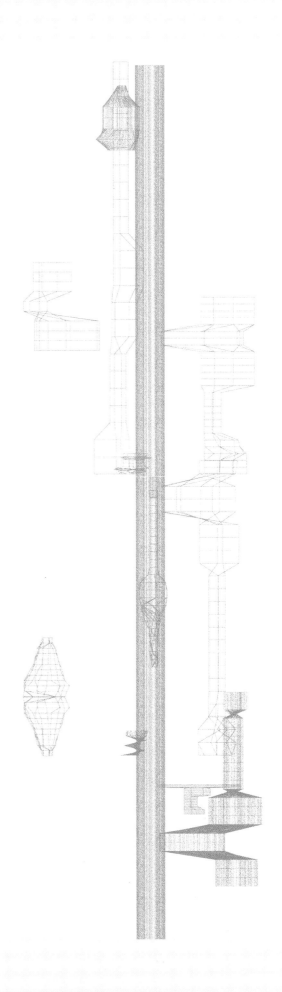

They claim that there are few reasons ever to leave the glasshouse since you feel as if you are inside the world, even though you are outside. If you want to, you can think of the house as a looking-glass that blocks out views and allows you to experience the world vicariously as a superficial interiority.

When the wind blows from the sea, the houses are transformed into the glasses of a giant harmonica that can be heard from a great distance.

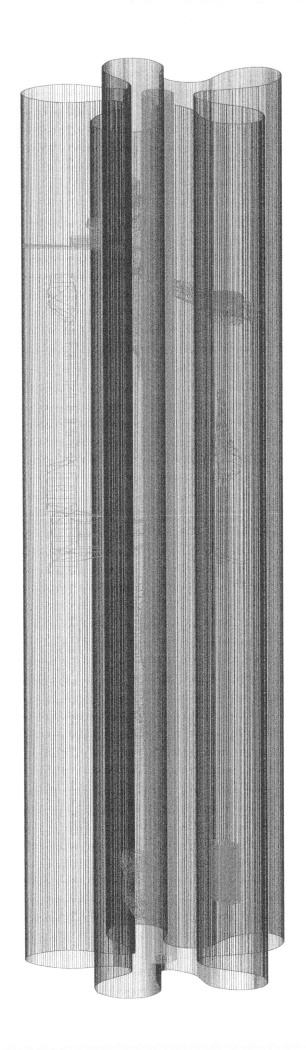

2.

Endings

Baritone solo

Trumpets 9

Horns 8

Tenor trombones 3

Bass trombone

Tuba

Tubular bells

Organ

Pianos 3

They can't be saved, since they die
the moment they've been fulfilled,
vanishing, as they came, into an impossible
hope for something that nobody expects.

A straight road that rolls on like a story
to its appointed end, with no digressions
other than the ones you imagine
in your longing to be surprised.

Afterwards it's clear which way they took;
you can't see them but you can hear the applause
from all sides: a –

–ni–mal night   sounds that

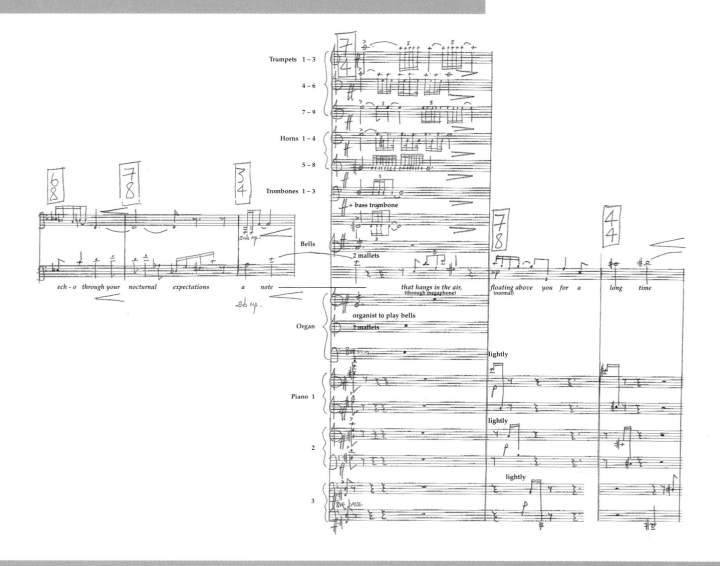

ech - o through your   nocturnal   expectations   a   note _____ that hangs in the air,   floating above   you   for   a   long   time
(through megaphone)   (normal)

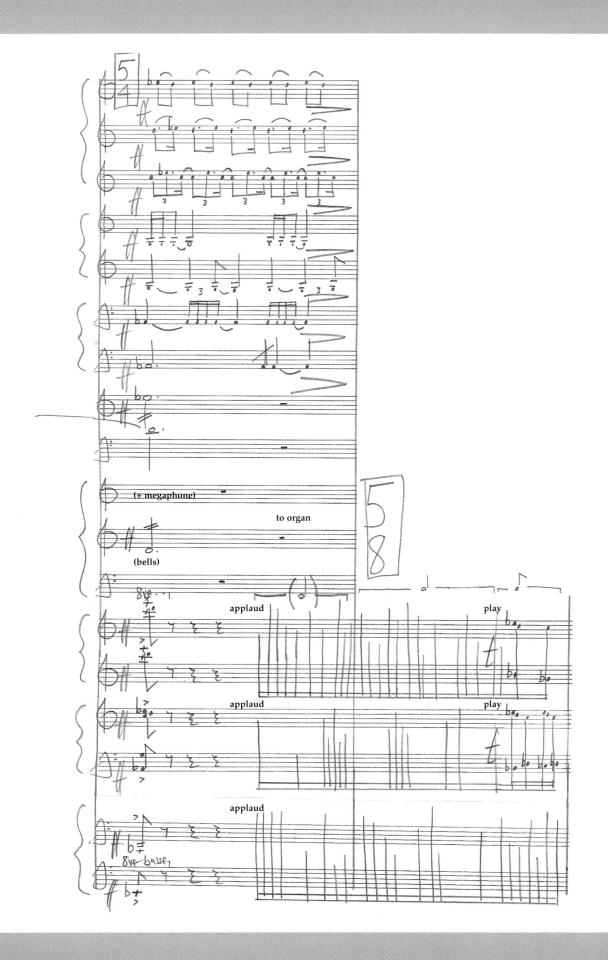

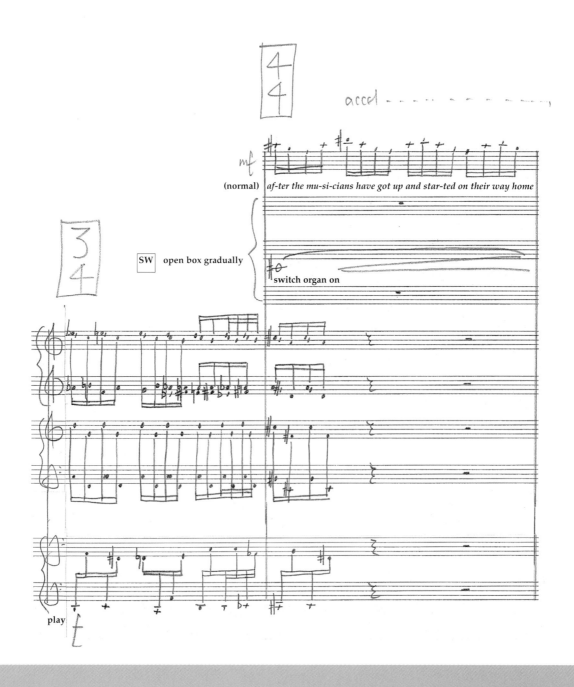

(normal) *af-ter the mu-si-cians have got up and star-ted on their way home*

SW open box gradually

switch organ on

play

All brass players except trumpets
1 and 4 to chant the following.
Pitch approximate. Tone rough.

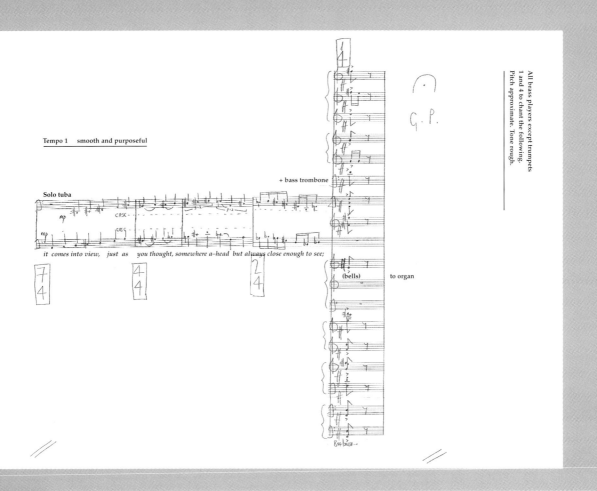

Tempo 1   smooth and purposeful

Solo tuba

+ bass trombone

(bells)   to organ

it comes into view,   just as   you thought, somewhere a–head but always close enough to see;

Solo

Trumpet 1

Trumpet 4

call   it home, it doesn't matter, because the end   is never just a word

black beads you   finger round a   string

roughly

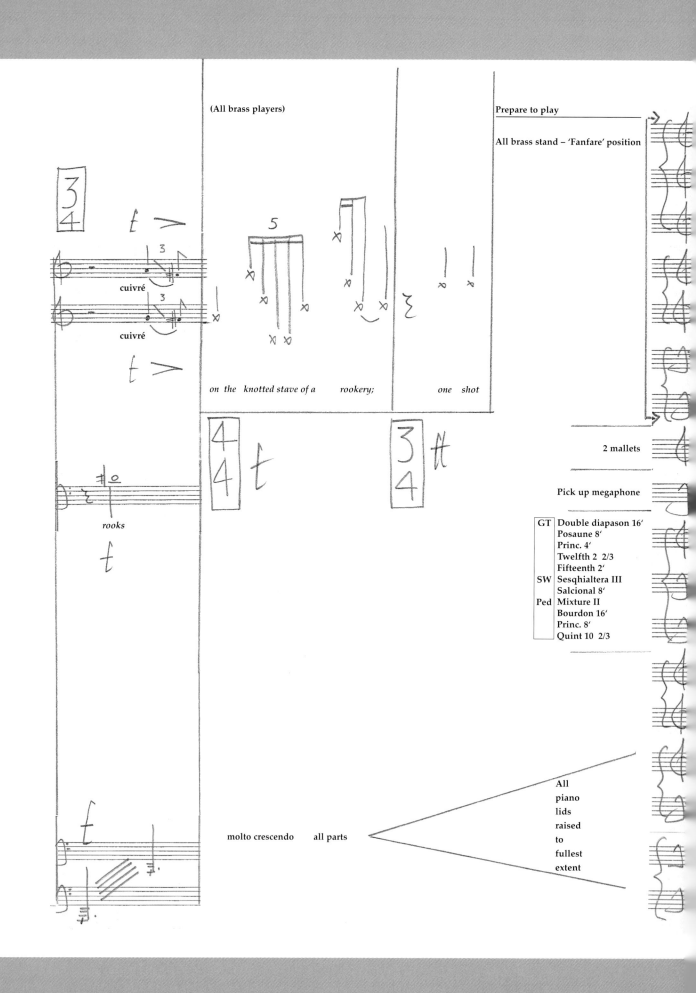

(All brass players)

cuivré

cuivré

rooks

on the knotted stave of a   rookery;   one shot

molto crescendo   all parts

Prepare to play

All brass stand – 'Fanfare' position

2 mallets

Pick up megaphone

GT	Double diapason 16'
	Posaune 8'
	Princ. 4'
	Twelfth 2 2/3
	Fifteenth 2'
SW	Sesqhialtera III
	Salcional 8'
Ped	Mixture II
	Bourdon 16'
	Princ. 8'
	Quint 10 2/3

All
piano
lids
raised
to
fullest
extent

and they'll take flight
leaving your hands free to applaud.

A tip where we throw everything
that's not needed; a mirror
where we empty ourselves of ourselves
to recognise the people we can't see.

She read the end of a
story before she started
it because who'd want
to be so easily disappointed?
If only she could have,
she'd have lived her
life backwards, moving
unexpectedly into
the present from a future
which was secure
because she'd been there.

BRE
RO

THE FULL
STOP HELD
HER STEADY
IN THE CHOPPY
SOUNDS

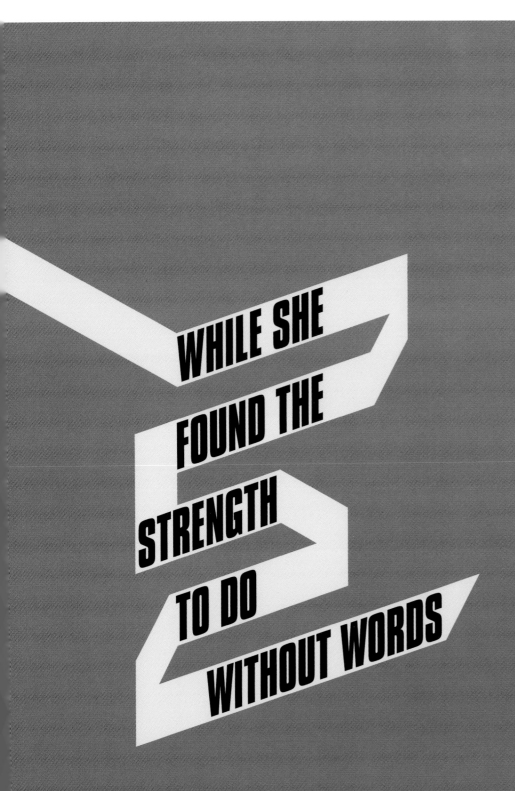

WHILE SHE FOUND THE STRENGTH TO DO WITHOUT WORDS

That's how she began: with the certain knowledge that the deadline had been met and the end could never betray the beginning.

For others it was a place they were heading, tearing through the city with only one thought in mind: would the ending come before the story had finished? It was the last station on the line. A get-away car that wouldn't start but warned the world they were trying to get away. A hook to catch an unlikely future if it passed by. A knot in a loopy necklace they'd picked up in a junk shop. An object that had begun with one use and ended with another but somewhere inbetween may have been valued for itself.

The silence as the credits rolled and they wondered where they were. A wall against which they sounded off their objections to a life that was only possible because they had to imagine it happening somewhere, sometime soon, before it was too late to make sense of the present.

For those people, the
beginning was an ending
that couldn't be valued
because it hadn't
happened yet. 'An ending
we're glad we've reached',
she might have said,
'is really a beginning'.
She knew that there were
as many ways of ending
as there were of beginning,
but most things ended
before they began.
Her conversations were
candles burning at both
ends from dawn to dawn,
from sunset to sunset.
Everything she said was
a means to an end that had
been postponed so that
she could say it.

Meanwhile she devoured
words to reach the full
stop that held her steady in
the choppy sounds while
she found the strength to
do without words. Feelings
ended when she said them
but she could talk herself
into feeling anything for a
moment, at least.

She knew that the world
didn't begin where she
ended and a happy ending
was an ending that was
endlessly beginning: the best
endings were those that
didn't finish.

1.

They clatter through the century like tin-cans on the back of a 'Just Married' car. They are one of the great inventions of modern times, with the machine-gun. Twentieth-century wars would have been impracticable without them.

They sustained an Empire, preserving an order in the midst of disarray. Explorers took them on expeditions to deserts where nothing grew except the expectation that one day cultivation would be possible.

In unhomely places where inedible food was served by untouchable hands, they were indispensable provisions.

They ensured that nothing was seen before it was ready to be consumed.

2.

The first meat to be canned, in Deptford, was named after a butchered woman: Sweet Fanny Adams. Something died with the tin; something was born: the tin-god of cosmopolitan modernity, process.

Fast, inscrutable, anonymous, encased like a bomb to withstand violent shock, food was a commodity that circulated around the globe.

It gave strength, like Popeye's spinach, enabling people to eat comestibles they would never have dreamed of eating before.

The bodies that ingested their packaged contents never had to meet the bodies that produced them. But like the undisciplined urban crowds which were consuming them, tins were dangerous.

They were disassociated and no longer rooted. Who could be certain of what the ravenous crowd was devouring? Something invisible and foreign might be inadvertently swallowed. This was colonialism in reverse: the haunting of the coloniser by the unfamiliar which he imagined he had annexed.

3.

The tin came to stand for modern, mass culture. People had begun to read rubbish, and they were eating it too so that their degeneracy had become visible. The democratic ideal of the indiscriminate tin that provisioned people, whoever and wherever they were, came to be replaced by the idea of the tin as unserviceable, junk food.

The tin stood for an emptiness that no political will could fill. It connoted an effortlessly and meaninglessly recycled process that engendered cultural products whose end was always unscrupulously commercial: canned-music, canned-laughter, tin-pot.

The tin was packaging without contents, a symbol for the shallowness of modernity and the heartless in modern culture. Remember the tin man in The Wizard of Oz who is on a quest for a heart to fill his rusting hollowness.

Some things cannot be preserved.

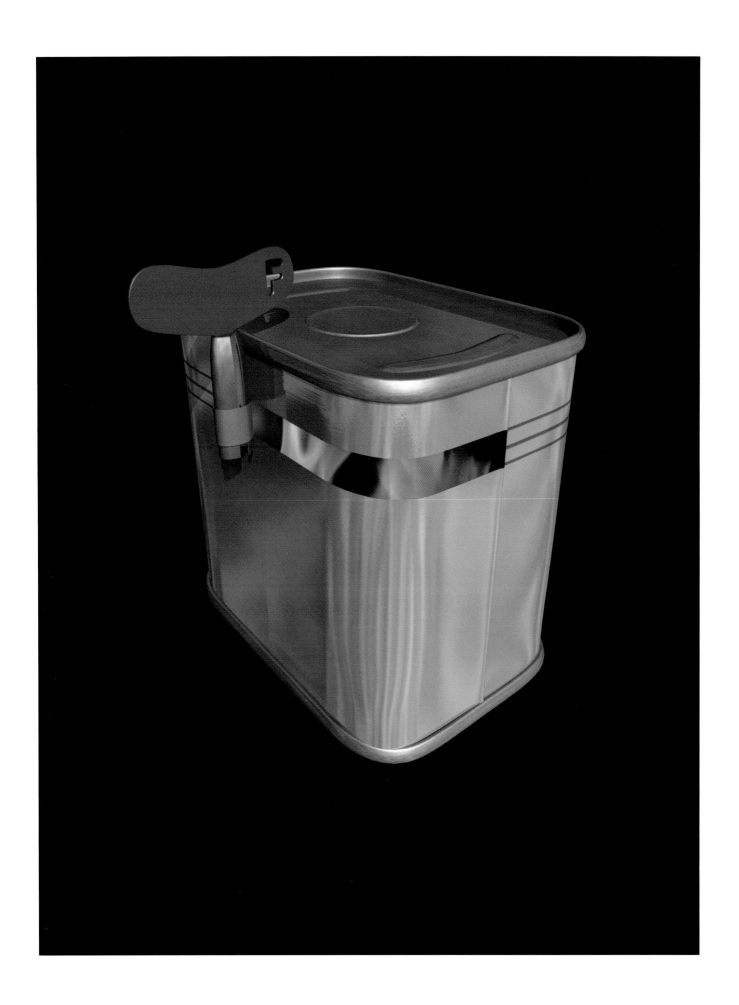

Memory is the That has been buried To be

Memory is a book that has been learned
By heart; the calloused hand
Of an archaeologist that touches
An object as if he had made it;
Or a gardener who shakes
The earth off the long roots
Which he has forgotten planting.

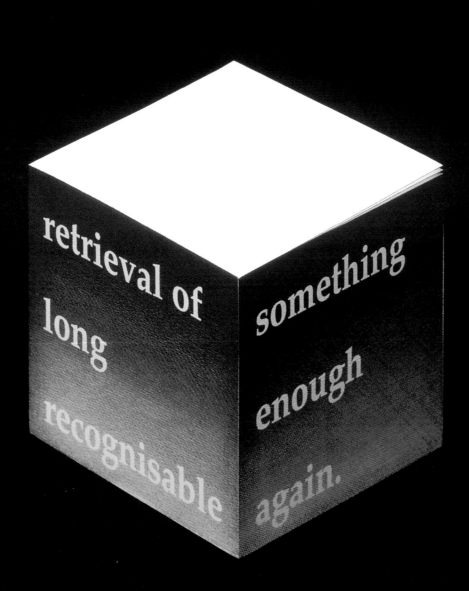

Memory is the recognition
That we only forget the things
We wish to remember.

Everything is an aide-memoire
For something, even if
We can't remember what it is.

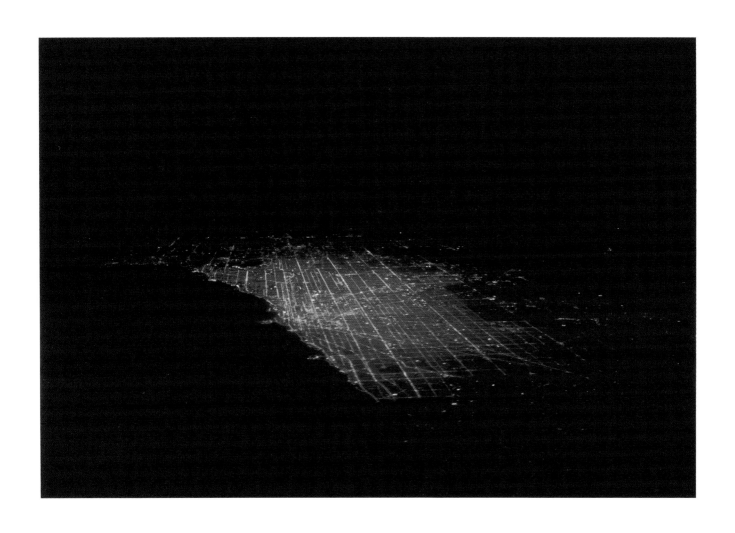

3.

Translation

A medical cure that is hit upon in the defective manufacture of another remedy

A word mismanufactured into poetry with a slip of the tongue

Can
I
Own
Myself?

THE NEED OF A
CONSTANTLY
EXPANDING MARKET
FOR ITS PRODUCTS
CHASES THE
BOURGEOISIE OVER
THE WHOLE SURFACE
OF THE GLOBE.
IT MUST NESTLE

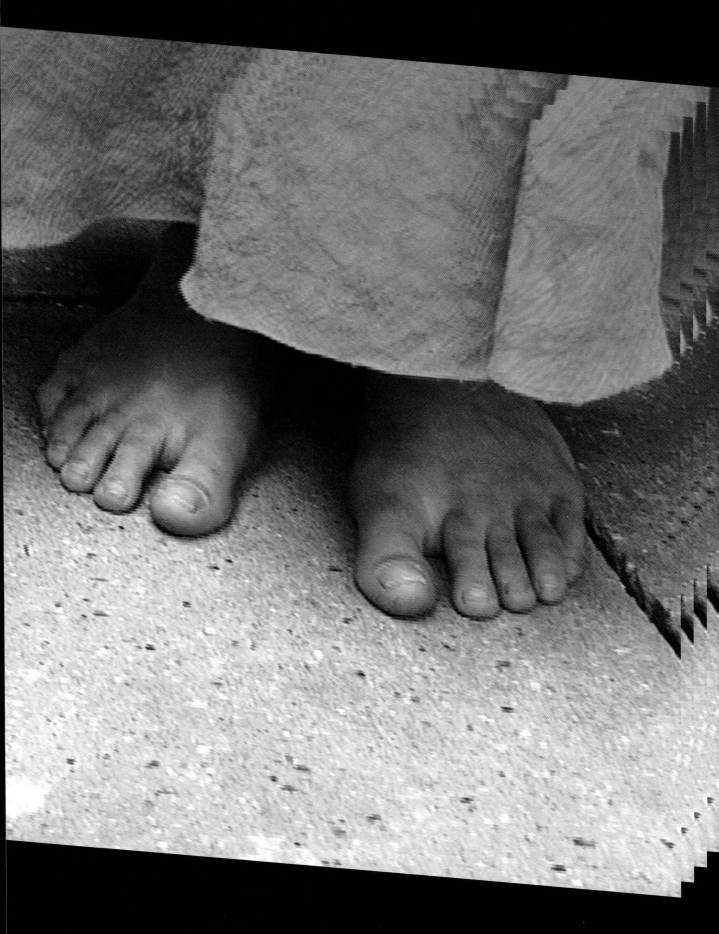

AN IMAGE IS AN ICON; A MATERIAL WONDER-WORKING
PLEDGE TO THE IMMATERIAL THAT HAS NO PERSPECTIVE
AND IS REVERED. WHEN YOU REPEAT A FAMILIAR WORD
OVER AND OVER AGAIN IT BECOMES FOREIGN.
SO TRANSPARENCY IS AN ILLUSION, AND MIRACLES MIGHT
BE HIDING IN OUR FLUENCY. IF YOU LOOK AT AN IMAGE
LONG ENOUGH IT BECOMES ANOTHER IMAGE.

An image is a shadow that is cast into the world, a net thrown out to catch slippery, wet dreams.
You can tell the time from the way the shadow falls, stretches and shrinks.
Sometimes the shadow flowers like a cactus blooming in the desert and people stop to clap.

An image is a sign of the times and a sign is a hot,
breathless tango danced by the sharp-suited signifier and
the voluptuous signified across the crowded ballroom.

An image is a picture which obscures its own history
behind the unequal histories of its spectators.

An image can make another image, like money makes money,
it can also cancel out another image, as money can lose money.

We kill the images we love and love them more for being dead.

A word, sound or smell can be owned—
an image— but can a gesture,
a way of walking, talking, smiling?
can I own myself?

A word, sound of smell can be owned—
an image— but can a gesture,
a way of walking, talking, smiling?
Can I own myself?

A word, sound or smell can be
owned— an image— but can a
gesture, a way of walking, talking
smiling? Can I own myself?

Imagine a time when images weren't authored, when nobody asked to know who was speaking; images circulated like words, in anonymity. What difference does it make who is speaking? (these words aren't mine.) The I of the poem was any voice that was speaking it. The I of the image was any eye that was looking at it.

Are we defined by the objects we hunger after or do we define the objects?

Desire is always a desire for ownership but some things can never be owned even though they are desired. Like desire itself. The value of the image resides in this contradiction.

You can't own the things you consume, but only those you produce. But you can consume the things you own. And to produce new forms, old forms have to be consumed. Nothing can be owned completely, because nothing is without history.

Ownership is linked to the rise of the individual as a unit in a political system; to be registered, checked, conscripted, sentenced, silenced - but also to be defended. One person's freedom is not another person's freedom. To own an object is not to own another object. Ownership, like freedom, is an invisible dispossession.

All that is solid melts into air,
ALL THAT IS HOLY IS PROFANED, AND MAN IS AT LAST COMPELLED TO FACE WITH SOBER SENSES, HIS REAL CONDITIONS OF LIFE, AND HIS RELATIONS WITH HIS KIND.

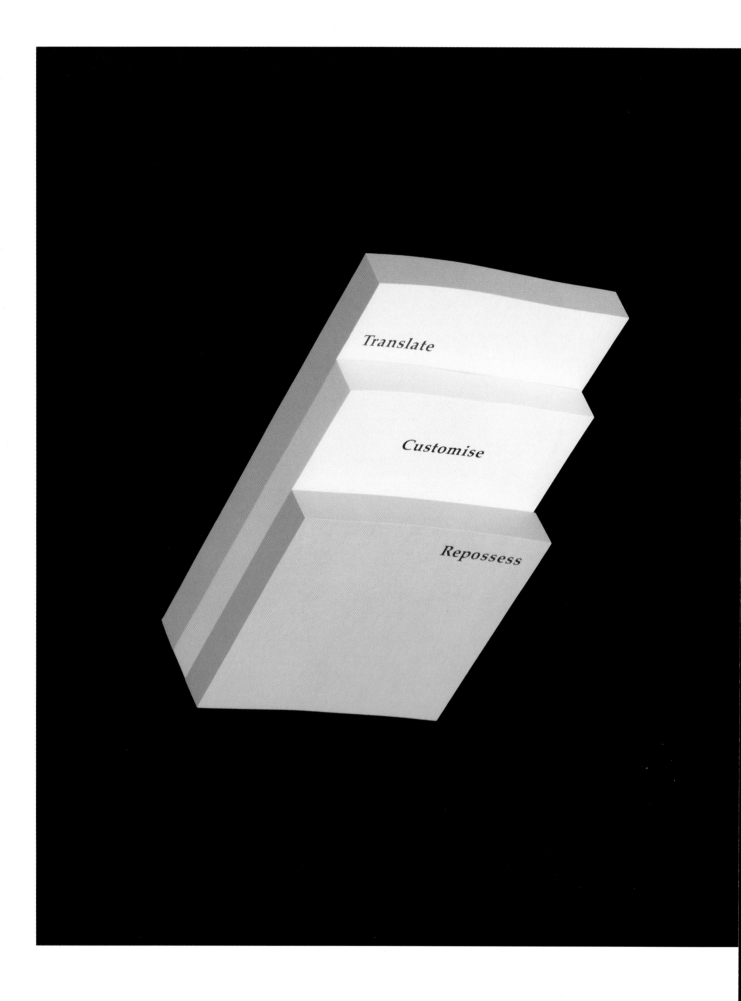

This is work dressed as play, a pack of wolves in sheep's clothing. They mean business, flapping on the white pages like bubble-gum anoraks that readers wear so they won't get lost on the walk. They are sweet–toothed tongues sticking out of a ravenous mouth, desperate not to be bookish. You can spot them from a distance, punched by the waves, like buoys above a diver who has gone to salvage what he can. They are a trail that somebody has left and if we learned to follow it, we'd be led back to a world without trails; the letter and the postbox in one. They are signs that the driver puts up when his vehicle breaks down and he leaves for help.

Or the cartoon shape that is drawn around a body before it is lifted away for examination. They are the places that some people avoid, and others hunt for, the shallow imprints of a history that walks are built around. Perhaps they were caught in the undergrowth or somebody fixed these markers to remember that something had been lost or found.

These signs were left here for a reason, which we have to guess. Sliced out of a map, they tell us where we are, when we're nowhere.

OCT.

DEC

NOV.

3rd Quarter

SEPT.

AUG.

JULY

2nd Quarter

NE

MAY

R.

1st Quarter

FEB.

There's a price to be paid for every rejection and acceptance.

You walk out of the room like a polite interruption that everyone pretends not to notice. The first thing you remember are the things you forgot to say and will never have the opportunity to tell. It's like a joke that lost the uproarious moment it fitted inside and has to be ditched among the hoary cha-cha of serious conversations.

How you are the only person who could give them value,

how you changed the course of history on your own when the others had gone home, how you can speak so many languages that everybody understands, no matter who they are, no matter where you are, how one day you will be where they are sitting and they may be where you were sitting. These answers were the public secrets that you waited for a private moment like this to disclose.

Then you count your blessings that you bit your tongue.

In your mind you are your own perfect interviewer, so you wonder whether you would recognise the signs of a rejection. The cap doesn't always fit: either you weren't right for the job, or it wasn't right for you. It's a natural process. Think of it as a foreign tissue, or a transplanted limb that your body has sloughed for reasons of its own.

Rejection is not a state that lasts for long;

it's the punchbag that you exercise your strength on to show the world what you are made of: a golden opportunity. It takes strength to accept a rejection and when the dirty business is over you can always launder your messy answers for another day.

29 30

25 26

27 28

23 24

3rd Quarter

21 22

19 20

You've already told them what they wanted to hear, so they've been cultivating their spiky, green assumptions on the cold mountains of paper. You walk into the room, a small-town cowboy who's bluffing his way into a bigger story. The doors of the saloon swing behind you like an applause that arrives at the wrong moment.

Everyone turns to stare except the people you've come to find.

They don't recognise you after all the things they've asked you to write about yourself. You guess what they are about to ask and they guess what you haven't said, looking in for the right answer, tossed to the bottom of an exhausted transparency. You've got seconds to show your mettle, but suddenly every plan you had is paper again. Your body wants to move, but it's keeping quiet inside a suit that smells like the stale mouth of your unlovable wardrobe. You shake hands, you look each other in the eye and wonder how you came to be in the world.

They pull tricky questions off their starched, white cuffs.

They've got to ask you what you know, which is more than enough: how far you've come to be there, how difficult it is to be judged when you're used to judging, how just when you're about to give the right answer something comes to interfere, how there are a million ways to be politely rejected,

but you'd rather be rudely accepted.

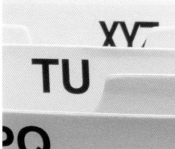

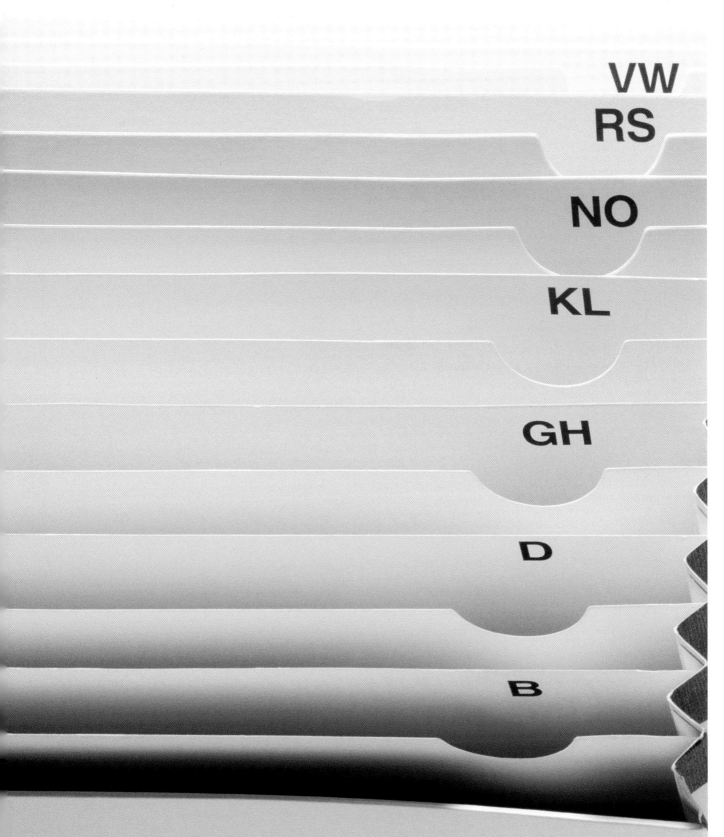

The doorway becomes an entrance or an exit depending on which way it swings, so you had better be prepared. It's already too late when you remember that rejection and acceptance are two different ways of pronouncing the same word. It is as small and fragile as a YES and a NO. Acceptances are displayed, like engagement rings

inside the sleeping boxes of their own rejection.

An interview is a box you have to fit inside and if you don't, you have to pretend that you do. Lop a bit off yourself here and there, twist a bit here and there so that you come out conveniently box-like. In the process perhaps 50 percent of you – perhaps even more – is lost. You're like the nylon showgirl in the magician's box whose impairment is only an illusion.

Interviews are events you dress up for, with your best suit and tie to stop you from falling apart.

An interview would be a conversation if the power were equally distributed. From a distance it looks as if the interviewer is conversing with the interviewee, the way that a man who is crying gives the impression that he is laughing, or a woman, seen from a moving train, looks as if she is running when she is standing still. An interview is the privileging of an impression over certain knowledge.

An interview isn't like a picnic that can happen anywhere; if it could, nowhere would be safe to talk. It needs a beginning and an end, a solid floor to wheel out the trolley of fluid questions and answers.

An interview is the possibility of everything going wrong and everything going right. If it had a colour it would be black and white.

An interview works through intentional misunderstandings.

An interview is a setting for remembering and forgetting model answers: strength of character, enthusiasm and the ability to work in teams; a capacity to take personal initiatives but also to delegate; over stretching, perhaps, and perfectionism, but determined to find solutions to problems and an ability to think laterally when it is necessary to do so.

An interview is the conversation over the counter of a shop that's been turned inside out and the buyer has become the seller.

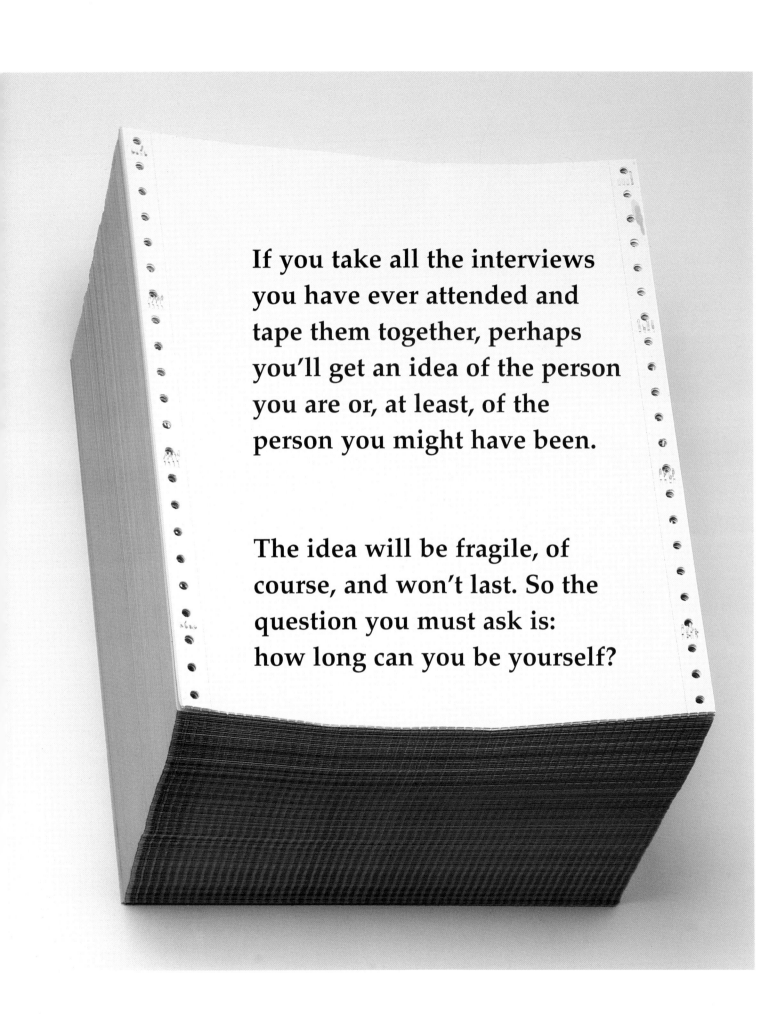

If you take all the interviews you have ever attended and tape them together, perhaps you'll get an idea of the person you are or, at least, of the person you might have been.

The idea will be fragile, of course, and won't last. So the question you must ask is: how long can you be yourself?

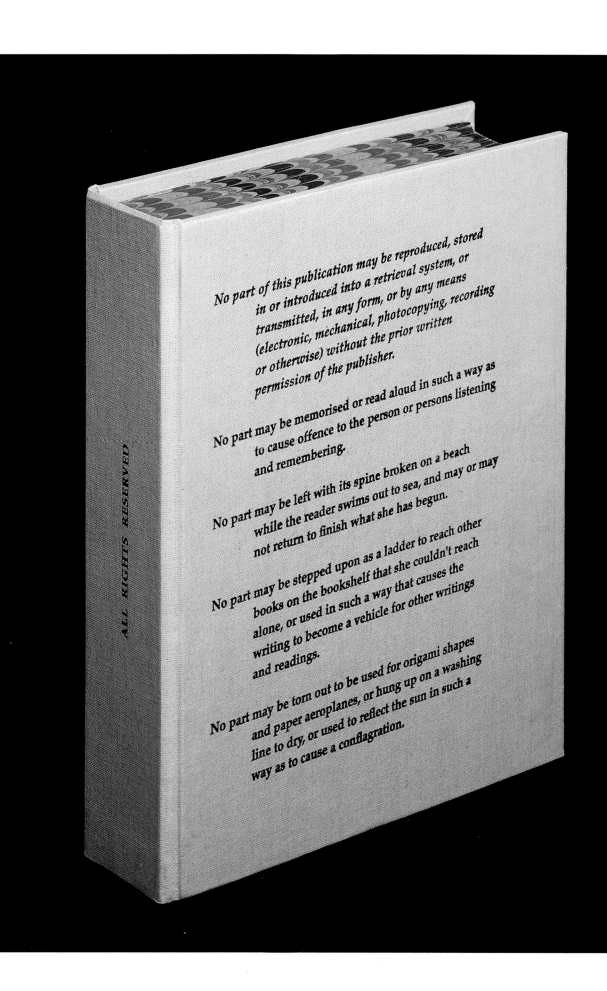

No part of this publication may be reproduced, stored in or introduced into a retrieval system, or transmitted, in any form, or by any means (electronic, mechanical, photocopying, recording or otherwise) without the prior written permission of the publisher.

No part may be memorised or read aloud in such a way as to cause offence to the person or persons listening and remembering.

No part may be left with its spine broken on a beach while the reader swims out to sea, and may or may not return to finish what she has begun.

No part may be stepped upon as a ladder to reach other books on the bookshelf that she couldn't reach alone, or used in such a way that causes the writing to become a vehicle for other writings and readings.

No part may be torn out to be used for origami shapes and paper aeroplanes, or hung up on a washing line to dry, or used to reflect the sun in such a way as to cause a conflagration.

No part may be used to signal to those who are living close enough to see but cannot hear, or if they do hear may be likely, for whatever reason, to misunderstand the words that are being spoken.

No part may be chewed over and over until it disappears back into the pulpy wood from where it came, leaving nothing but the acerbic taste of a message.

No part may be used as an envelope to store letters or the petals of dried flowers, or bank notes that are left and forgotten until the currency passes out of usage and they're rediscovered with a new value.

No part may be used as material to seal an absence of whatever kind and of whatever size, even when a life depends upon filling the space.

No part may be used as a press to flatten a living moment into a page, or as a weight to keep down an object that might otherwise fly or move unimpeded as a book moves through the hands of a reader.

No part may be intentionally, or unintentionally passed over in the race to reach the end, or when the end is reached, may be used to qualify the finality of the conclusion.

No part may be walked across, or in any way trespassed upon other than those parts that are clearly marked as affording safe passage through the plot.

No part may be used, implicitly or explicitly, as assignations for those too timid to speak their mind, or to be seen for what they are.

No part may be looked upon as a mirror that reflects back the person of the reader, or the space where the reader should be if she was free to look.

No part may be reassembled in any order other than the order imagined by the reader when she wishes that the story had ended differently.

No part may be used as ballast to keep a vessel upright, even when the vessel is unstable and might easily capsize.

No part may be used as a fan to keep cool when it is too hot to read, or to stoke a fire where it is too cold to read.

No part may be used as a clock to tell the time by the pages or words, or for any other kind (whatsoever it may be) of time-telling.

No part may be used as a buffer to shield the reader, or as an object of aggression with which the reader may cause injury, or grievous bodily harm, to a person other than herself.

No part may be wantonly fingered in any way that may cause misunderstandings to arise or may suggest a familiarity where no such intimacy exists.

No part may be coveted or valued above any other part, so that the wood is overshadowed by the tree.

No part may be used as a recreational or resting place for any other person or object other than the eyes of the reader as they pause on their walk.

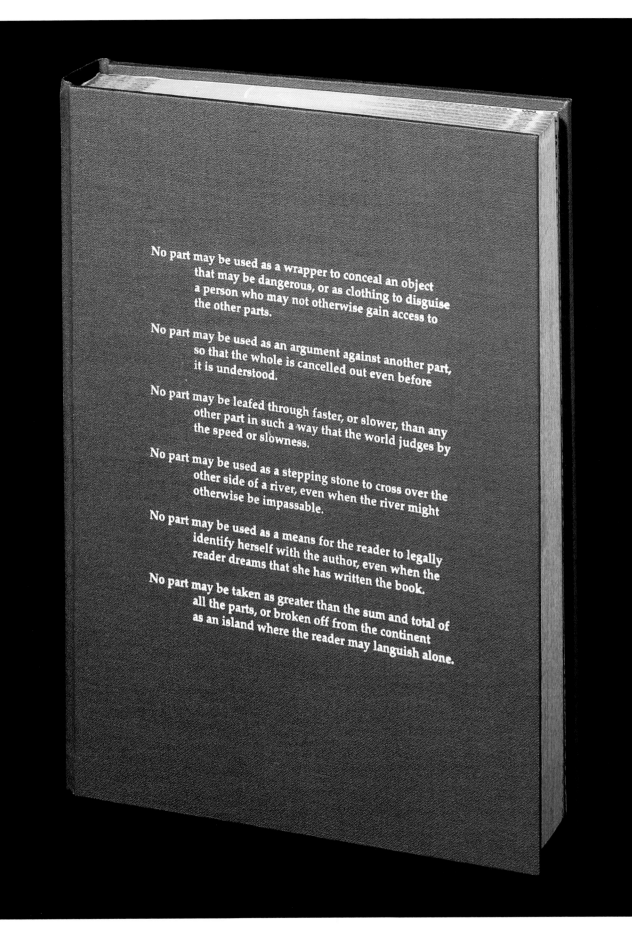

No part may be used as a wrapper to conceal an object that may be dangerous, or as clothing to disguise a person who may not otherwise gain access to the other parts.

No part may be used as an argument against another part, so that the whole is cancelled out even before it is understood.

No part may be leafed through faster, or slower, than any other part in such a way that the world judges by the speed or slowness.

No part may be used as a stepping stone to cross over the other side of a river, even when the river might otherwise be impassable.

No part may be used as a means for the reader to legally identify herself with the author, even when the reader dreams that she has written the book.

No part may be taken as greater than the sum and total of all the parts, or broken off from the continent as an island where the reader may languish alone.

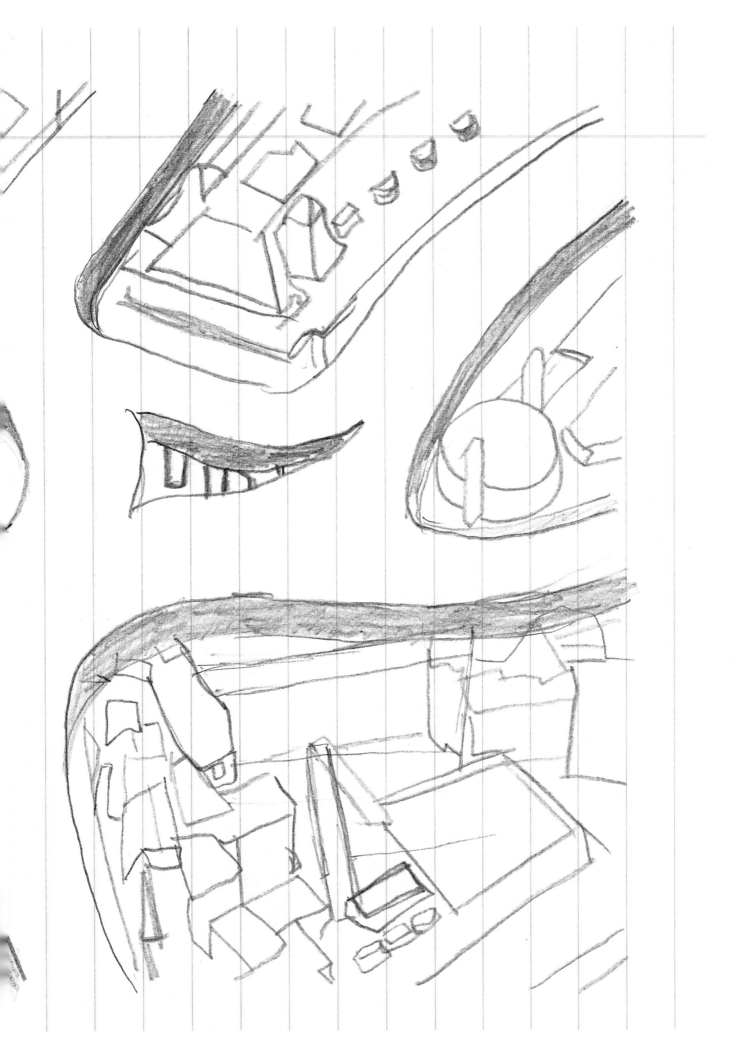

131

The road is a line that
gathers stories as it moves forward,
straightening the uneven
past for an acquiescent future.

It's a visible solution to the
insoluble problem of trafficking;

a whip that's cracked
above the urban recalcitrance.
A tie around the puffy neck
of the city fat man.

Roads are built
you want to go,

to by-pass the places

working obsessively
against the
lie of the land.
They are the plot lines
in a school-book
that have been
taken out for exercise.
Roads are raised up
on pedestals
or go walking through
the city on stilts,
like a solstice
on the back of a
monolithic
priesthood.

They are strands of
been carefully
spaghetti that have
playing unashamedly
disentangled by a child
Roads are the markers
with her food.
the snakes that
on a board game,
on his ladder with
tempt the climber
without
imaginings of a place
roads.

Lights could be dangerous, but it isn't safe to remain in the dark. Either way, it's a risk. If they're on, they'll be able to see me, and if they're off, it's impossible to prepare. Some houses have automatic lights that operate themselves, so when the lights come on you know the people are out. They aren't stupid, they know about light and darkness and they know about silence. It's what a drowning man hears when heavy hands hold his head down and force him out of the world he wants to hear.

Sleep is dangerous because they'll take advantage of you, and you never know where you might surface. Take every chance they can to slip in when the lids are down. It isn't safe to be lulled into a watery silence. They're behind the walls. Tiny sounds inside, like rustling mice, except that these aren't mice. The clatter of people trying as hard as they can to suppress the noises they make. And now, the sound of ice cracking. Maybe hands flexing, getting ready to spring out of a handshake, or eyelashes brushing against the partition as they watch.

They've planted a device, a magnet vacuuming sounds. Breathing is difficult when you know your life depends on it. They'll hear the effort of each inhalation, the muscular contraction of every dry swallow.

Where is it? Behind the television screen in the corner, a stagnant pool where they try to camouflage their secrets with the green scum of the room's reflection. There's more than one. The telephone is hooked up and listening to things it shouldn't be listening to. And I'm listening to the telephone listening and it's a question now of patience.

BLIND SIGHT
can only be framed in hindsight when we have matched the object we knew was there with the object that we can finally see.

You can hear
this sound waves
echoing back from
the depths of
unconsciousness
like a radar
scanning for stealthy
dorsal images

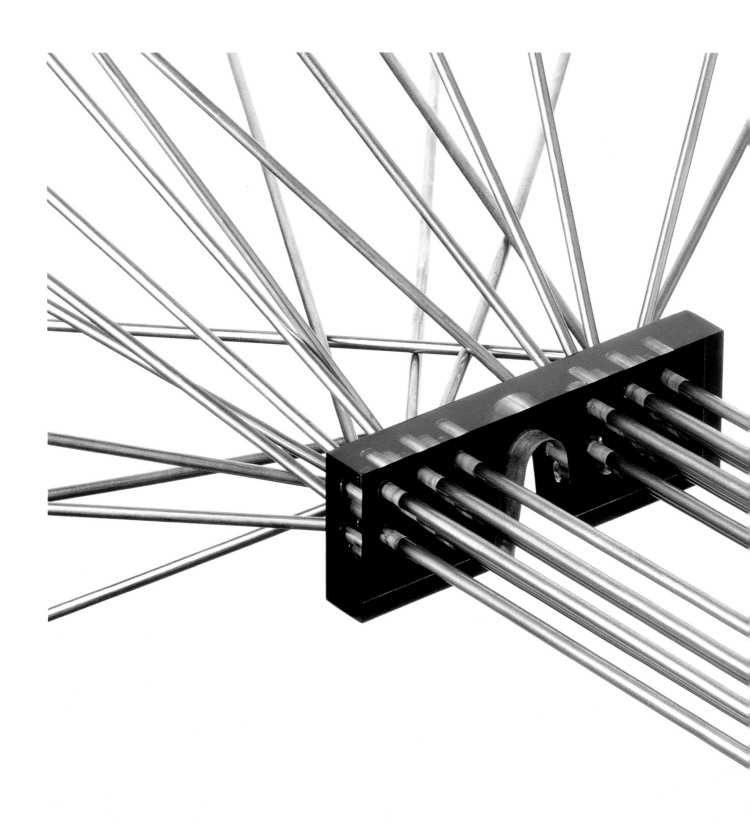

The eye is a cohesive window that objects stick to until the pane is full and nothing more can be seen behind the visible blind. Still, you can make out a lot from the shadows that walk past and don't try to behave themselves because they imagine they are not being watched. You can feel they are there, pushing against your sleepy body, reminding you of all the things you thought you hadn't seen.

This blindness is more than the absence of sight.

The last space in
the puzzle is the pool
where everyone
wants to paddle until
the moment comes
for another sight to
pull the plug on this
madness and show
us the world as it was
intended to be.

Peter Miles

Damon Murray

Stephen Sorrell

Face values are often the right values on the face of it. Chin, mouth, nose, cheeks, eyes, forehead: they're the pegs that fix the surface sheet of this faceless anthropometric regime where the body is measured, described and exposed in the dark room.

ter Miles

Damon Murray

Stephen Sorrell

No face is identical, so the descriptive portrait becomes a way of identification. To lose face is to come face-to-face with yourself in the face of this danger of being somebody else. When the singular name's been hammered out into flat, polished body parts, nobody cares about the mechanical intricacies inside.

Peter Miles

Damon Murray

Stephen Sorrell

ter Miles Damon Murray Stephen Sorrell

Sometimes you ask how people
had the face to call themselves after
you, but there's no need for an
answer, because your face is there
to prove the difference.

Art direction **Miles Murray Sorrell (Fuel)**
unless indicated*

Contributors

Pierre d'Avoine Architects *55-59, 61*

Tim Beer *25, 27, 28, 31*

Diana Burrell *72-79*

Matthew Donaldson *14-19, 33, 37*, 41, 42, 46-47, 49, 52-53,*
92, 93, 105-107, 109, 118, 120-129, 148-149, 156

Annabel Elston* *54, 60, 80-81, 84-87, 90, 91, 136-139, 142-145*

Toby Glanville* *62-69*

Frederike Helwig* *6-9, 12, 13*

David Spero* *94-101*

Andrew Stafford *49-51, 148-149*

Juergen Teller *110-111, 113, 114-115, 116*

Thanks to

Lily Donaldson *130-131, 134-135*
Lucinda Gresswell *33*
Andy Martin *105-107, 109*
Kate Moss *110-111, 113, 114-115, 116*
Red Post Production *89*

Peter Miles, Damon Murray and Stephen Sorrell
have worked together as a graphic design group
since 1991. They produced seven *Fuel* magazines
before their first book *PURE Fuel*, published in 1996.

Shannan Peckham writes on cultural politics,
design and film. He is the author of *National Histories,
Natural States* and editor of *Heritage: Cultures and
Politics*. He is a Fellow of St. Peter's College, Oxford.

3 0 3
3
3

1